ANGELS
Success and Prosperity

Become a Mover and Shaker of Your Reality

the Angel Lady Terrie Marie, D.Ms.

Angels Success and Prosperity

Copyright © 2017 the Angel Lady Terrie Marie, D.Ms. All rights reserved. No part of this publication may be reproduced or transmitted in any form or by any means, electronic or mechanical, including photocopying without written permission of the Publisher. Any unauthorized use, sharing, reproduction, or distribution is strictly prohibited. It is illegal to copy this book, post it to a website, or distribute it by any other means without permission from the Publisher.

Limits of Liability and Disclaimer of Warranty:
The Author and Publisher shall not be liable for your misuse of this material. This book is strictly for informational and educational purposes only.

Cover Design by Tovar Printing
El Paso, Texas

Book Design by Bluebobo

Distributed by
Angel Lady Aurora, LLC
El Paso, Texas Unites States
© 2017 – All Rights Reserved WorldWide

Dedicated to ~

My Family and Friends for your
unwavering support and encouragement

Students and Clients for giving me the gift of
sharing my knowledge and experiences with you

LightWorkers, Spiritual Leaders and Healers
I have met along the way

Mentors, Teachers and Coaches who have helped me stand
in my truth of who I am and what I came here to do …

and to
My beloved Angels and Divine Source
~ the Angel Lady Terrie Marie, D.Ms.

the Angels Lady Terrie Marie's Mission Statement:

Inspire, encourage and support beautiful Souls round world-wide to seek their Life Purpose, raise their vibration, experience massive mind-sets shifts, create their personal 24/7 relationship with their Angels and their Inner-Intuitive Self attracting more opportunities, clients and taking their success and prosperity to the next level and beyond.

Contents

Preface 1

CHAPTER ONE: Eight Ways Spiritual Entrepreneurs Measure Success and Prosperity 9

    Angel Prince Melchizedek 15
    What Defines Success for You? 16
    What Is Prosperity to You? 20
    Angel Barakiel 24

CHAPTER TWO: Who Are You Being? 25

    Are You Holding Yourself Hostage? 28
    Angel Saterel 30
    Are You Hiding or Showing-Up for 31
    Your Dreams? 31
    Angel Elemiah 35

CHAPTER THREE: Are You Stepping into Your Value? 37

    If You Are Whispering Nobody Can Hear You or Your Message .. 39
    Angel Uzzah 42
    Are You Afraid to Be Seen? 43
    Angel Zuphlas 45

CHAPTER FOUR: Fear Freezes All Your Assets 47

    Does Fear Drive You into Submission or Propel You Forward? ... 49
    Angel Nathaniel 51
    How Fear Scams You into Giving Up 52

Angel Chairoum 53
CHAPTER FIVE: What Is Your True Reality Really? 55
    Your Inner-Game VS Fear = Manifestation 56
    Archangel Uriel 59
    What Does Your Inner-Game Really 60
    Manifest into Your Life? 60
    Angel Asaph 64
CHAPTER SIX: What's Next? 67
    What If You Could? 69
    Angel Haziel 70
    Transformation from the Inside Out is Crucial to Your Ultimate Success and Prosperity 71
    Angel Ezekiel 74
Next Steps … 75
About The Angel Lady Terrie Marie, D.Ms. 85

Preface

Talking to Angels is part of my nature in the same it is effortless to breathe without thinking. Most people refer to their talents, skills and unique gifts and abilities as 2nd nature to them.

When we allow ourselves to accept that which makes us uniquely brilliant as part of our nature, we truly have taken that Leap into Faith, knowing there are stones to place our feet upon or we're going to be given wings to fly effortlessly.

It wasn't always this way for me. I used to be afraid of my own shadow, preferring to hide in the corner rather than be noticed and certainly NOT fully seen!

It took many years to accept who I am and what I came here to do before I could even begin to express the messages of Angels through me with confidence.

The path we travel has so many twists and turns it is simply not possible to know everything until it is fully revealed in that moment of being fully and completely aligned with the truth of where you are on all levels of vibration and belief.

On a bright sunny, beautiful day in July 2010, it started just like so many others. It was a busy day Border Patrol Agents coming in, 18 wheelers delivering goods and equipment to be unloaded and inventoried. Then in less than 20 minutes, my entire world as I knew it was turned upside down, inside out and twisted beyond recognition!

You see, in those 20 minutes, I was laid-off from the position I held for more than 9 years as an Executive Administrative Assistant AND escorted off the premises as if I had all of a sudden become a liar and thief. In between the tears streaming down my face in utter shock and disbelief, I started thanking my Angels for looking out for me and protecting me from what I wasn't able to see at the time.

Less than 24 hours later, I received what I was told was going to be an exit interview. Turns out Corporate informed me I was now fired and was UPS overnight, express delivered a termination letter clearly stating I was not re-hirable. To say my head was spinning at this new development is an understatement.

I had known for a while that at some point I'd be completely self-employed doing what I am doing now. In the meantime, I had been setting money aside and had started my Holistic Healing business working nights and weekends.

August 1, 2007 is the day I applied for and received my business license for Desert Rose Healing Arts. Giving Angel Readings and Angelic Light Weaving fed my Soul and I loved connect to Angels in this way. My favorite part was channeling essential oil blends, creating a wide variety of Aromatherapy oils and a line of beauty products. At one point crystals were introduced to this eclectic mix to encourage manifestation, healing and raising inner-vibration for my clients and customers.

Even though the learning curve was incredibly steep and the hours very long, I was in heaven.

Circumstances beyond my control had thrown me into the deep end without a safety net … or so I thought at the time. I learned to swim superfast … it was made incredibly clear I was to forge a new path and it wasn't getting another day job. Even in those darkest moments, I just knew I had to take that next step no matter what it 'looked' like.

A mere 2 months later, on September 29, 2010, I published my first blog post. It literally took me 10+ hours to set-up my first blog and figure out how to post something to it. Before I knew there were 'techie Angels' they were helping me honor a commitment I made to myself and my growing online community. It was to be the first of countless steps onto and into the worldwide web, becoming visible and walking my path in a way I had never considered. Had I known what was truly being asked of me, I would have not only firmly slammed the door; I would have nailed and tapped it shut to make sure it stayed shut!

Fast forwarding a few years, I studied and studied, cried, stumbled, struggled and quit more times than I care to count or remember.

Opportunities to teach classes about Angels, Angelic Light Weaving, Reiki, chakra's and crystals started showing up. In less than 12 months from that fateful day in July 2010, I had somehow started mentoring people around the world and teaching classes online.

I learned how to grow and nurture a business, write articles and working finishing my first eCommerce website. My mom saw me writing books and encouraged me to add to my credibility by earning my Doctorate of Metaphysical Sciences degree which I earned May of 2012.

Listening and follow my Mom's advice was one of the best decisions I've made. The time and effort it took to start and accomplish my Doctorate, helped me have confidence in myself, my skills, talents and innate ability to connect with Angels. It also confirmed and validated a lot of what I just *KNEW* were truths without ever having formally studied metaphysics.

I read book after book trying to figure things out like how some people are able to manifest anything and everything they want, when they want it and … why so many others struggle to make ends meet.

Make no mistake; I was among the many who struggled to manifest a consistent flow of financial prosperity.

The conscious mind is tricky and devious. I fell into every trap along the way to discovering how, exactly how I was holding myself in a pattern of lack, limitation and delay. Yes, there were many glimpses of the 'financial prosperity promised land' and then the seemingly inevitable would happen … that awful snap backwards experiencing the never-ending cycle of feast or famine!

Then there was the hiding-out part that kept in that place of not showing-up for my purpose of being here in the first place.

I didn't really want anyone, except my closest friends to know that I actually talked to Angels AND they were 'talking' to me through intuitive thought, energy and visual and audible cues.

In the summer of 2015, July 5th to be more specific, the laptop I had been using for several years decided to transition, crashing and taking with it *EVERTYHING* from the previous 5+ years of work. I was devastated. It would be 5 weeks before I was once again back online. That was the deepest, darkest time I can ever remember experiencing in this life-time.

By the Grace of God and the patience of my Beloved Angels, I was able to find the light once again one step at a time.

At the time of this writing, it's now 18 months later and I experienced a financial re-birth, giving the house I owned, back to the bank. There was an emergency gallbladder surgery too.

Lessons have been learned in the most unusual ways, revealing yet another part of the overall plan for my being here in physical form at this time and in this place.

I have come to understand hiding behind a mask prevents the Light within to shine wholly and completely without regard to what is said or thought by others.

It is about allowing the natural flow of financial prosperity to manifest through me consistently, matching not only my desires, also being commensurate with the vision given to me by my Beloved Angels in service of others.

My Beloved Angels help me help myself find the courage to show-up in ways I never imagined. There are times, even to this day; that I take several deep breaths at what is being shown to me and the guidance being received in taking that Leap into Faith yet again.

I am often asked how Angels have and do help me with my business. The question is important on so many levels, involving both the conscious and sub-conscious minds respectively.

It has been more than 15 years since I made a conscious decision to stop trying to *'fit in at all costs'* among the un-awakened, sleepwalking Souls. From the moment that decision was made, everything changed almost overnight, some of the changes were expected, while others were not.

I did *know* most of the friendships would simply dissolve and fall away. For a time, my biological family and I were estranged. We have since healed and now have an amazing relationship as a result of that breaking away from old, hurtful roles and patterns of behavior.

Everyone has their unique path and the ways in which Spirit, Universal Energy and Angels help them with their lives, goals, dreams, relationships, career and businesses. Here's how my beloved Angels help me throughout each day …

- program and course titles and the content for each
- writing emails giving value and promoting webinars and various programs
- channeling all my books, including this one
- finding things that I may have misplaced
- guide my every step
- recognize opportunities and discern the difference between those that are a good 'fit' and those which are not

It's all about blending the Spiritual and the physical ream, knowing when to take action and when to remain silent. This book --- Angels Success and Prosperity --- is part of the overall vision of helping as many people worldwide connect with their Angels, raise their inner-vibration, attracting more opportunities, clients and financial prosperity.

Make no mistake, without financial prosperity, no dream, no goal and no life purpose can be fully and completely realized.

There is no doubt, more shall be revealed to me and through me in the days ahead. In the meantime, hiding and playing small is no longer an option nor is it acceptable. It is about walking my walk, and walking my talk more authentically and transparently than ever before. There are more lessons to be learned, healed and released so that I may continue to reach out, giving a hand-up to many hundreds of thousands of women and men round this world.

The intention and purpose for having shared all this with you, is to help you along your unique path no matter how many twists and turns attempt to distract of derail you along the way to fulfilling your purpose and experiencing success and financial prosperity.

Much Love, Light, Peace and Prosperity,
the Angel Lady Terrie Marie, D.Ms.

"Words are the true measure of what you are feeling, seeing and manifesting in the world around you."

CHAPTER ONE:
Eight Ways Spiritual Entrepreneurs Measure Success and Prosperity

"Until you are fully aligned, you are not fully expressed."

Success means different things to many different people, from all walks of life. For some, it is about being able to live in peace and harmony with the land. For others it is having massive amounts of money at their fingertips. For still others it is all about power and being powerful.

Here are a few more ways success can and often is measured:

* status symbols in the form of luxurious homes and furnishings
* designer labels
* earning 6 and 6-figure incomes
* the number of people on a mailing list or Social Media

followers
* being able to travel to exotic places
* climbing the corporate ladder
* knowing one's Life Purpose
* Best-Selling Author

It could also be about being able to live in a country and in a manner of one's choosing. We are all gifted with free will, the gift of choice. For many people round the world, simply being able to choose is the ultimate form or measure of success.

When I ask my clients and students what success is for them, most have never truly thought about this, much less given serious below the surface consideration to what success is or what it looks and feels like.

So many people have been told that to be Spiritual is also about not wanting to have money except to cover their needs. It is an unwritten rule that to be Spiritual one must choose not to have anything in excess, especially money. Money is often seen as evil and makes people corrupt.

There is nothing that lowers one's vibration more than to wonder and worry where the next client, job, opportunity or dollar is going to come from. A truth is, when you worry about how to make ends meet, all you think about is money … how much there is and worrying if you can pay the rent of put food on the table.

How beautiful Soul, does lack feed your Soul or help you do what you came here to do? It doesn't.

Here's part of what defines success for me …

… Being able to host the Success and Prosperity Mastery Interview Series, creating a platform for amazing, gifted and talented entrepreneurs from all walks of life expressing themselves and lessons learned along the way.

It also helps many others find the courage to find their own voice. Lessons, challenges and obstacles are part of the Journey Less Traveled ... the way of the courageous in-Spirit requires us all to step out beyond everything we have come to know, trust and believe keeps us safe and insulated from doubt and fear.

The interview series also helps position me on the leading edge and as the 'go to Angel Lady' in the Spiritual Community. Even putting that into printed words, causes me to take several deep breaths, quieting Ego-chitter chatter attempting to call me out as vain and egotistical.

The more I choose to show-up, the more I can be of service, helping others along their Journey Less Traveled.

... Being able to set aside time each week to channel this book with the intention of reaching thousands upon thousands of beautiful Souls round this planet.

Each and every person, including you, has something special to offer with the rest of us. Most of us have shamed, taught or worse ... bullied into remaining silent. Silence in this instance, is certain death for the sharing of your unique message with the world.

Let it be said yet again here and now ... your voice and your message need to be heard more now than ever!

- Being able to take the time for personal retreats, to re-connect with my inner-intuitive self and re-charge my Spiritual energy from the inside out is paramount to continually up-leveling my inner-vibration to the next level and beyond.

- Stepping away is one of the ways I give myself permission to be in the silence, connecting with Mother Earth and beloved Angels. Taking a break is essential for personal and Spiritual Growth and letting go.

- Being able to step into faith is for me an incredible success milestone. I used to worry about how to pay bills and be able to invest in growing my business. Several months ago, September 2016, I received clear guidance during a Skype meeting with my webmaster. You see, I was thinking of opening an online Crystal Shoppe. The guidance was to specialize in one-of-a-kind pieces. Mind you, the Tucson Gem and Mineral Show was still 5 months away.

This also meant having a significant budget to invest in this venture I was clearly being guided to pursue. I love crystals and have a few hundred or so round my home, home office and in my meditation gardens. Seven years had passed since I had been to the Tucson. I used to write articles about crystals teach Crystal Healing Classes and sell crystals and tumbled stones.

This is where stepping into faith comes in, because intuitively I knew what the budget was to be. It was a bit scary as I was rebuilding financially after experiencing major surgery just 6 weeks earlier.

My beloved Angels have always been there for me, even in the darkest of moments. It is in having and stepping into faith which allowed the financial budget to manifest *AND* have more in my bank accounts too! Following guidance, I was able to recoup 2/3 of the initial investment, including travel expenses in just 2 days of the soft-opening of our online Secrets from the Crystal Garden Shoppe.

What defines success for you beautiful Soul? Be willing to go below the surface of what the conscious mind tells you it should look and feel like for you. Perhaps success is earning 6-figures or multi-6-figures. Or landing a promotion, living in your dream home … maybe even teaching others how to connect with Angels.

ANGELS SUCCESS AND PROSPERITY

What truly defines success for you? Be willing to go below the surface of what the conscious mind tells you. Perhaps success is earning 6-figures or multiple 6-figures a year. Or landing a promotion, living in your dream home … maybe even teaching others to connect to Angels.

Speaking of Angels, the first Angel to join us along this journey of *Becoming a Mover and Shaker of Your Reality* is one of my longtime Angel Companions, Melchizedek. This powerful Angel continually helps me step out beyond what is commonly referred to as 'the comfort zone.' He helps me find the courage to follow the path as it is revealed to me.

No matter what your purpose or path is, it's all about repeatedly stepping out beyond everything you have ever known and gotten used to doing, saying and becoming. Sometimes Melchizedek's energy is or feels brutal in his frank-no-nonsense messages and guidance. At other times, his energy is subtle, like a benevolent big brother keeping watch … you know … just in case there's a 'stumble' or unforeseen obstacle. This is when, if you have been heeding guidance given you're given a hand-up to see the bigger vision that is waiting for you.

Here are a few of the many ways Melchizedek helps you, beautiful Soul …

- Protect you from stumbling and getting discouraged on the path that's in front of you
- Make the right and best decisions for you, your business and your Spiritual Path
- Guides you to the right people to help and support you as the next steps are revealed

Melchizedek is one of the most powerful Angels. He is also known as the Angel Prince of Peace. He is the Angel of Spiritual Growth and Expansion. He also specializes in mentoring Spiritual Entrepreneurs to become more of who they are deep within.

In order to grow and expand Spiritually, one of two 'states of being' need to occur ...

#1: A great sense of peace flowing through you as if there is nothing and no-one external to you that can possible disrupt or distract you from your path. It's a feeling that is best described as floating in trust and faith. It is in the silence, you prepare to receive guidance, messages and confirmation about a plan of action you are about to put into motion.

#2: Descending into a state of great upheaval like being laid-off or discovering and coming face-to-face with beliefs that no longer serve you or your highest and best good on any level. This can feel like everything is unravelling or spiraling out of control right before your eyes and there doesn't' seem to be anything you can do about it.

No matter which 'state of being' --- peace or upheaval --- you are experiencing, Melchizedek will help you navigate the seemingly treacherous energies of transition and ultimate transformation.

This magnificent Angel will help make decisions from a space within you laced with unconditional love and compassion. He will most definitely help you start, grow or expand your business.

You need only ask for his help to discern the difference between inner-intuitive guidance and conscious-mind Ego-chitter chatter. Once you have 'asked,' be open to receive and trust what is being given to you. If you're unsure if what you're getting is really from Melchizedek --- ask --- ask for confirmation. It's better to ask for clarification and confirmation than to assume what you're getting is from your human-self and disregard it as unworthy of your attention!

Angel Prince Melchizedek
A Reflection of What Once Was

Child the great sorrow you travel through is simply the
reflection of what once was and is no longer.

It is the deep cleansing and clearing that must take place as a
result of all you have done to create new patterns within your
conscious mind through the sub-conscious.

The sub-conscious is where the power lies. It is in the place
where dreams come alive with power, unconditional love,
compassion and indeed a sense of forgiveness.

The trials are a result of human resistance not yet uncovered. It
is in these moments of great cleansing that one can then begin
the ascension process towards inner-enlightenment.

With Ascension, you are given great opportunities to create
space on a grander scale in making a difference
in the lives of others.

Make no mistake, it is in this place, this state of being, that all
things are re-borne, re-newed, re-awakened.

Be compassionate with yourself as the demons will attempt to create havoc so as to turn you from those who love and support you.

Know I am with you in all moments even when it feels and appears to be the exact opposite.

In truth, you are never alone as you are
All-One with Spirit and all of my brethren.
Know this to be truth. Embrace the truth of all that you are no matter outward appearances to the contrary.

You are being prepared for greater works than these.
We are complete.

What Defines Success for You?

At first glance, defining success seems rather straightforward. After all, who doesn't truly want to be successful? True, there are a rare few who claim that 'success' is only for those privileged few, whose who are destined for greatness which the vast majority are not.

Success is different and unique for everyone. No two people are exactly the same, similar in many ways, yes. The exact same … no. every journey has countless twists and turns even when it appears, from the outside, to be a fairly straight, clear path.

It can be elusive, this thing called success because so many fail to take the time it requires to go below the surface noise spewed by the conscious mind, Ego-chitter chatter. When 'asked' what defines success for them, most respond 'off the top of their head' without even pausing for a moment to breathe.

These are typical 'off the top of the head' answers I've heard thousands of time from clients, friends and family alike:

* live in peace
* get a job or better job
* figure out and live their purpose
* happiness, they just want to be happy
* have better health
* be in or heal a love relationship

You may be wondering what's wrong with those answers. Well, nothing except the answers are very generic responses when someone asks questions about being successful.

The definition of success is: the accomplishment of an aim or purpose; the attainment of popularity or profit; a person or thing that achieves desired aims or attains prosperity.

It is something that often seems as abstract or intangible because the interpretation of success is person and different for everyone. There are as many facets to defining success as there are facets on a diamond. A few of the many facets of success include, but are not limited to …

  … status in a company; being on a Board of Directors
  … highly visible position in the community
  … level of education and degrees
  … size of an email list
  … level of income; the number of zero's
  … property; where or in which area of a city / town one has property
  … designer labels on clothing, accessories, vehicles
  … publishing a book or several books

... traveling to beautiful places
... iving one's purpose
... being asked to speak at events
... being of service, teaching, coaching or mentoring

It can be several things. It is all encompassing and the secret is being willing to go within to discover what it really means for you. One way to do this inner-reflection work, is starting with your dreams. Here are a few questions to help you get started:

1. What is it you most love doing?
2. What do you want your life to look like?
3. Where do you want to be in 6 months?

Get out of your own head-space, going below the surface of the conscious mind and into you're your heart-space. Take a few moments to write out the answers to the three seemingly super-simple questions in the previous paragraph.

Most people are afraid to actually put a name to their dreams of being successful because they don't want to fail or they don't have any true support to help them when there's a rough patch. And there is always a rough patch!

Sometimes a 'rough patch' lasts only a few moments, hours, days or perhaps a few weeks ... or longer. Extended 'rough patches' are also known as a Dark Night of the Soul where everything appears to be or is falling apart round you. Nothing seems to be going right no matter what you do or how hard you work.

In the summer of 2015, I experienced an incredibly intense 'rough patch.' The laptop I had been using for several years, died, taking with it 5 ½ years of work with it, including my first major Angel book (Sacred Angel Realms). I was crushed, withdrawing from everything and everyone. It was so dark; I didn't think or feel I'd ever see the Light again. It would be 5 weeks before I was back online. Little-by-little, my beloved Angels showed me where to recover information, files and anything else that was needed to re-birth me and my business.

Since that intense period of transformation I have …

* published 3 books, all of which are Amazon Best-Sellers
* given the house I bought entirely on my own, back to the mortgage company
* downsized to a beautiful spacious, 2-bed apartment I truly enjoy
* healed my relationship with my biological family
* re-invented my business twice over
* experienced emergency surgery

Here is what defines success for me --- it will probably morph yet again, but for now --- being able to live my purpose freely in harmony and peace. It's about following my path, hand-in-hand with my beloved Angels and being in-tune and attuned with both my Inner-Intuitive Self and my Higher-Self.

Success is showing-up, continually stepping into my value, being of service at ever increasing levels of vibration, creating and holding space for my clients and students to experience massive mindset shifts and transformation from the inside out as we 'dig-out' the *Blind Spots*' which disguise the Core Wound, re-programming the conscious mind. It's also about being financially prosperous in ways that no only support me and my ever expanding business, but also enables me to work with amazing people around this world which in turn, helps them fulfill their dreams.

So beautiful Soul … what defines success for you?

The first step to release blockages to achieving and experiencing continued success, is to go within, asking what would change for you. The next step is to commit to doing what you know and are guided to do, to achieving the level of success you yearn for deep within your heart and Soul. The third step is to be willing to be comfortable being uncomfortable, taking the necessary next steps, no matter how scary, by stepping into faith.

Did you get clarity around what defines success for you? If not, please stop and do that for you, your dreams and goals. It will give you the clarity needed to increase financial prosperity.

What Is Prosperity to You?

Prosperity shows up in a wide variety of ways, sometimes showing-up in very unusual and interesting ways. It's not always possible to predict how or when prosperity shows up.

Just the other day, I received a check for $54.45! It was completely unexpected and very welcome. Extra money is always welcome and I 'celebrated' this happy surprise with a huge smile saying thank you about a dozen times. Look at the numbers … 54 … 45 … both are 'repeats' and are '9' a sign of completion … a cycle of completion can gift you with such a sense of release and freedom.

Here are just a few of the ways prosperity can show-up in your life:

* check in the mail or refund
* pay raise, if you work for someone else
* finding coins on the ground

* a cup of coffee or treated to a meal
* time with a dear friend or loved one
* a new set of linens
* a bonus session with a favorite coach or mentor
* a scholarship
* a sale at your favorite store / shoppe

Financial prosperity can also arrive disguised as a phone call, email or text message inquiring about your products or services. Whether or not the person who contacted you actually books a session or orders a product, be sure to say 'thank you' for the sign of manifestation. If you're not careful, conscious-mind Ego-chitter chatter will turn such instances into negative energy which only causes lack and delay, restricting the natural flow of prosperity.

On the occasion when someone doesn't show-up or cancels, I always say 'thank you' seeing it as a gift of time. That wasn't always the case. I used to get upset, sometimes wondering what I did to cause the no-show or cancellation. In part, I was responsible because my inner-wealth thermostat was set very low back then. Getting upset only served to keep my inner-wealth thermostat low.

It wasn't until I figured out how I was tripping myself up, was I able to really turn that around. It took practice to re-program the conscious mind because it was hell-bent on going down the same worn-out rut of negative thoughts and emotions of not being good enough, deserving, worthy or worse being punished for some long-ago screw-up.

Prosperity is about more than financial gain. It is most assuredly measured by the balances in bank and investment accounts and in your pocket. The primary or one of the primary measures of success is one's bottom line ... is there more money coming in than going out? If not, what are you willing to do to increase the inflow of money and still bless the outflow?

Believe it or not, there was a time shortly after moving from Hawai'i to El Paso, Texas, when my monthly income was $600 a month. Yup, that's it. It was very humbling to be in a situation where I was living with my parents for an extended period of time – 6+ years to be more precise. There I was a grown, independent woman with 'house rules' who had been on her own, married and managing a household to suddenly being divorced and barely able to make ends meet. It was awful and yet having a roof over my head was a blessing.

During those 6+ years, I learned how to manage the resources I had, buy a car and become debt free once again. Before moving from Hawai'i, I had a good job and had started expanding my own business painting tropical flowers and colorful reef fish on watercolor paper and canvas tote bags, supplying several prominent tourist shops in Waikiki.

When you find yourself not doing as well as you once were or as well as you'd like, it can really mess with you on multiple levels. Let's look at this for a moment ... when you feel like you're not getting anywhere or when bolls start piling up, it can quickly become overwhelming.

Being in a state of overwhelm about anything --- especially finances --- takes a toll mentally and emotionally. It becomes more and more of a challenge to keep one's inner-vibration from taking a nose dive and staying there.

Instead of staying in a place of judgment, blame and overwhelm, which only serves to keep your inner-vibration low, look at what you can start doing to first accept the current situation and then what steps you can put into action to change things in positive ways. It won't be easy in the beginning, but so very worth the effort, time and energy. The investment you'll be making is in yourself.

Part of the 'work' is about forgiveness … forgiving others as well as yourself. For this we turn to Barakiel, the Angel of Prosperity and Abundance.

Without forgiveness, there's only so much forward movement that can be attained and maintained. Think of forgiveness as your 'magic freedom key,' freeing you from an emotional prison designed to keep you from reaching the Light and stepping into the wholeness of you.

Angel Barakiel can become your guide and ally as you begin an inner-journey of healing like no other. This amazing, powerful Angel is part of the Seraphim, Angels of the highest vibration of all the Angelic Hierarchies. He will help you heal in ways that will clear your path mentally and emotionally, raising your inner-vibration.

Having and maintaining a positive outlook while undergoing deep transformation, is an essential piece to the whole process of letting go to gain more, increasing the inflow of prosperity and recognizing opportunities as they are revealed to you.

Barakiel can assist you in clearing outdated beliefs that no longer resonate or serve your higher-purpose. Feeling like you are sinking or barely holding your head above water is tiring, causing more struggle, lack and delay.

Everything starts by acknowledging where you are, where you have been and where it is you are now going. Make no mistake; there will be distractions and mis-steps along the way. As you become more in-tune with you, you will become more consciously aware, thereby choosing differently, creating new, more positive pathways of giving and receiving.

It is necessary only to acknowledge each step as it is revealed to you and taking action upon those steps immediately, without delay.

Angel Barakiel
Begin Within

As you begin the journey within your mind,
connect first with your eternal heart space.

It is here you will connect with your truth of love,
light and that of forgiveness.

See all who have harmed you as stepping stones to
where you now stand.

All that is behind you is to remain firmly, lovingly behind you
as you move forward towards all that awaits you.

Only in the Light of Love through forgiveness will you then
begin to see differently.

Seeing is the first step of reaping the rewards of manifestation
along your chosen pathway of prosperity.

Be mindful. Be grateful. Rejoice in all that is shown to you, all
that is being revealed and given to you in all moments,
regardless of surface appearances beloved child.

That is all in this moment beloved child of Light and Love.
Be not afraid you are loved beyond measure in all moments.

CHAPTER TWO:
Who Are You Being?

"The past is a reflection of who you once were and that which has become the stepping stones to all that awaits you."

Once a long time ago, in what seems like a different lifetime, I was given a gift by someone I cared for deeply. In the grand scheme of this life and the many twists and turns it has taken, the gift wasn't anything special except for its meaning to me. I kept it long after the relationship ended. It was a keychain. One end was cut crystal with a black leather strap.

This special gift had been dropped, glued back together twice and the edges were worn and chipped … it was rather banged-up. One day after looking at the pieces in my hand, having broken a third time, I knew it was time to release it completely with as much love and forgiveness as possible. I smiled through soft tears of what might have been and said 'good-bye.'

In those last moments, I realized that I too, had gone through many transformations. My edges were banged-up, there were scars from countless wounds that have long-since healed over the years.

The healed wounds and those that sometimes remain open create a type of filter or mask which we use to hide the truth of who we are. It is a fear of being hurt, rejected, criticized or even ridiculed for our beliefs and the purpose we seek to fulfill while being of service to others that keeps your light hidden in the dark shadows of what could be.

Admittedly, there are a few masks I seek to recognize, remove and ultimately dissolve. There are only a few left. Maybe, that too, will be a distant memory once the last word is written and this beautiful collaboration with my beloved Angels goes to print, finding its way to you.

The masks most of us 'wear' and hide behind are those that we see as a sort of refuge from prying eyes. We hide behind a façade of being 'fine' for fear of anyone … anyone would dare get a glimpse of our deepest fears and our deepest desires. Speaking from experience, I hid 'me' away so deeply it has taken what seems like two lifetimes within this very life, to re-discover, heal and allow the light to shine brightly through my heart and Soul once again.

There is one short story I'm being nudged to share with you … when I was twenty-something, while at a family gathering in Waikiki, I heard a relative say --- *"Look at her sitting there like the Queen of Sheba or something when she KNOWS I AM the Queen!"* it was all I could do to not run screaming from that moment. It felt like my eyes would give me away any second. My skin and my heart sank. No one knew just how keen my hearing really was. I know now I must have had help holding it all together.

Everyone, no matter the circumstances of their upbringing, has a few scars causing them to retreat into themselves.

There are many masks and many layers to uncover and explore, much like an archeologist on a dig in exotic places like the ruins of Ancient Egypt or Machu Picchu. When a 'discovery'

Is made, there can be a mixture of excitement and trepidation not really knowing what lay beneath the newly revealed mask. More than once I have thought --- and hoped --- this is it! I've *FINALLY* got to the bottom there's no more pain or ugliness to uncover and heal.

That is probably the most challenging aspect of being on this Earth Journey for anyone to come to terms with … there is always another layer lurking deep within … at least this has been my experience and that of all my clients. There is a sense of knowing, a deeper knowing of healing that can be experienced when we allow ourselves to go within so we no longer go without the light on our face, in our eyes which streams through our heart. Doing 'the work' is at times tedious, frustrating and heavy. Perhaps you have gone through a Dark Night of the Soul a time or two … this is a sign of massive transformation.

Massive transformation is Spiritual Alchemy in its purest form of Light peering from the deepest recesses of the shadows … the 'space' where the mask lives. The very mask or masks that seek to keep all of us small, ineffective and hiding out so we're not visible even to ourselves.

Do you recognize any of these masks in you?

* not being good enough
* undeserving of being prosperous
* fear of the unknown
* afraid to be 'seen'
* being unloved or unlovable
* feeling like a fraud

- fear of failure
- what will others think or say
- fear of success
- not special enough to …
- clueless

There are so many masks we've learned to accept as truth, condemning ourselves to carry as our own during this lifetime.

Isn't it time to put that burden down?

Are You Holding Yourself Hostage?

Everyone, at one time or another, has felt deeply hurt, been betrayed or had their heart broken maybe you, or someone you know, has been even been scammed. We all have scars and heart-wrenching tales of 'whoa' to justify our being closed off, frightened and just plain scared of showing our true self in the light of day. We're all taught many important lessons through fear and judgment … the cost of not-conforming to whatever society deems 'appropriate' for that particular time, place or situation.

Here's the truth about that --- in my humble opinion --- being 'closed off' is just that. It means exactly what it implies … being closed off from all that you desire and all you came here to do feel and experience in the living of your life and the sharing of your journey with others along the way.

If you are 'closed off' in any way, on any level, you will struggle with challenge after challenge to take that Leap into Knowing and Trust. It also means, it is scary to take advantage of the many opportunities that are constantly being revealed to you … many of which are exactly what you've asked for.

The good news is ... you are here; you've been drawn to this book and what's being shared within these pages. This shows YOU just how ready you are to move forward, stepping up to that next level of confidence, empowerment, success and prosperity.

Have you identified the masks and / or life experiences that have been allowed to influence who you are and limiting the way(s) you allow the world to 'see' you? If not, stop right now and list all the masks that come to mind.

The label or labels you identify with is an exact reflection of what and what is not happening for you. The way you 'talk' to you when no one is around, is the truth of who you think you are and what you deserve ... all that negative self-talk is the key to your inner-manifesting dialog.

What, beautiful Soul, are you allowing to define you? Does the past, the 'old broken' you define your present?

Before I started teaching online, I taught workshops in the homes of friends and a few local metaphysical shops. During one of these classes, one of the students was so filled with hurt and anger, I could barely teach the class. Her energy was filled with so much 'righteous bitterness' that it was stifling. I took several deep breaths and starting putting my things away to leave saying I wasn't able to teach the class with so much negativity and judgment. I got up to leave and was asked to stay. The energy softened enough, enabling me to stop clearing my throat Chakra and breathe easier. That beautiful Soul had been so deeply hurt and disrespected; she hadn't been able to get past the pain. It literally defined her entire existence for nearly 18 years!

I ask you again ... WHAT are YOU allowing to define you?

Perhaps Angel Saterel will give you insight into who you are and who you want to become on your way to living your purpose, experiencing success and prosperity along the way, in the manner you desire and deserve.

Angel Saterel
Dare to Dream

That which appears to be elusive,
is truly in front of you this very moment.

All is not so lost that cannot once again be found
within your heart, beloved one.

Dare to dream the big dreams of Soul Purpose for it shall
not be denied you by any other than of yourself.

The small keeps all things small,
out of reach beyond comprehension.

That which is behind you must be recognized now,
as part of the whole, lest you lose sight of your True Self
which is of Light and Love.

The past can only define what it is allowed to define.
Be prepared to free yourself from the choices that bind
your heart, mind and energy.

Free yourself with compassion, forgiveness and that of love.

Call upon me, now this moment,
to guide you through the inner-gift of seeing past
that which no longer resonates deep within.

Replace all with discernment, knowing all is indeed being revealed to you as you are genuinely open to receive all that has been asked.

You alone have the power to break the bonds of what is now behind you.

All energies are directed by your thoughts and emotions, beloved child of Light.

Step out and away and into your dreams more openly, more lovingly and more fully with each breath, with each step forward.

Look deep within to find the answers you seek. Call upon my brethren and me to assist you in discerning that which is of ego-mind and that which is of truth.

For only in the seeking of the truth shall you find the freedom you seek in all that compels you forward.

Are You Hiding or Showing-Up for Your Dreams?

April 2016, I applied to be a guest on the popular Coast to Coast Radio Show. I received a phone call as a result of the email I sent a few weeks earlier. The follow-up phone call interview lasted nearly 20 minutes. The radio show producer said 'she'd see what she could do to put me on the schedule.' It was an exciting moment and felt like the heavens had opened up big-time!

Well, 30 days came and went, then 60 days more without a follow-up email or phone call from the show's producer. It was disappointing and I also knew there was something else coming my way. What that something else would be, I had no idea. I did send a follow-up email and even sent a copy of Sacred Angel Realms to the show host. Silence followed. The 'message' was not now, maybe not ever.

In truth, I wasn't ready for such an opportunity. I thought I was. Looking back now, sharing this with you, it is clear, I had not yet fully found myself. Maybe we never fully and completely 'find' ourselves in this human life. When one does, it is then time for the Soul to depart back into the fullness of Spirit from whence it came.

You see, I was still finding the path of my purpose. Yes, working with Angels and sharing this with others but within this broad path, was a more focused path that had been eluding me. I was still trying to 'fit in' with the mainstream way of doing things. Sometimes it even worked. It was also rather confining and caused friction which presented itself as resistance and blocked the flow of literally everything.

Do you catch yourself stopping just short of taking that next step or taking a step or two backwards because of what others might say or think about you, your dreams and all you desire to accomplish along the way?

Sometimes all it takes is a seemingly innocent remark by a friend, relative or client and something gets triggered that makes you feel a bit guilty for going to your favorite coffee shop a couple times a week. In reality, the remark is more of a reflection of envy at not having the freedom to do more of what they want to do.

A lot of people who want to have a lifestyle of comfort,

financial prosperity and the freedom to do as they please, will remain within the safety of the 'comfort zone bubble' because it's what they know. There's no failure within the 'comfort zone bubble' except … the price of confinement is certain death of their dreams.

Every time, and I mean, each and every time you say 'no' because it's scary or you don't have guaranteed outcome, you hide from your truth and you deny those whom you came here to serve. This includes serving you and your purpose.

Just because you say 'yes' to trying something new and putting yourself out there, it doesn't mean it will be successful. There have been many times I acted on guidance only to have something not happen the way it was shown to me. What I didn't fully realize, was that I was the block. I was still hiding.

I knew something had to change in a very big way, within 7 days of that clear knowing; my physical body experienced emergency gallbladder surgery. I was forced to allow my body to recover for several weeks.

During that transformational healing, it was as if a 're-set 'button had been activated. I could no longer hide. It was time to show-up flaws and all, stepping into the Light more fully every day.

There have been a few setbacks here and there which served as reminders to re-connect and step into faith more fully and completely.

It hasn't always been easy. Anyone who chooses to follow their path as openly and fully as possible is certain to run into stubborn conscious mind resistance, and find themselves landing on their batukus from time to time. It's what you do next that matters. It is also very important to honor what you're feeling, allowing you to purge fear, doubt, frustration, disappointment, betrayal and even heartbreak or it will rise to the surface again and again until it is fully purged.

If you allow anyone, including you, to stop you from reaching out for what you truly want, you are literally allowing someone else to dictate your fate. Taking even one small, tiny baby step each day puts *YOU* miles ahead of sooooo many millions of others who are too afraid to take a chance on themselves.

It's about going within, making a decision and then doing what it takes to follow your Soul's path towards living your purpose all-in and all-out. You know if you're hiding or showing-up for your dreams. There is always something more you can do. For instance, you can start a gratitude journal, acknowledging all that you already have in your life. Gratitude raises your vibration, allowing you to see and recognize just how special you truly are, beautiful Soul.

This is where I'm going to out myself because I almost allowed Mercury Retrograde to stop me from accepting an opportunity that just 'showed up' less than 24 hours ago.

Allow me to back up just a bit. Today is April 18th and on April 2nd, I made a decision to myself and to my beloved Angels to re-commit to showing-up more fully, manifesting my dreams and being of service in a much more open and bigger way. This also meant I was agreeing to giving the most valuable, content-rich and transformational service I am capable of giving.

Showing-up, also means knowing when to admit you're not in the right 'space' energetically to give a client your full and undivided attention because your energy is *off*. Re-scheduling when you KNOW you're not capable of showing-up fully is in the best interest of your client(s).

If you now you are in a space of 'less than your fullness' do everyone the courtesy of re-scheduling. You cause more harm by being dishonest with yourself and believe me, people will know! I've had that happen to me more than once

Always honor where you are in the moment. It speaks volumes about who you are. Your actions and your energy precede you.

When you notice your energy, thoughts or emotions being out of balance, take time to go within and connect with Angel Elemiah, Protector of All who go within, re-connecting with your inner-intuitive Self.

Angel Elemiah
Persistent Faith

It is imperative dear one to seek balance within your core.

All is revealed to you during moments of silence.
When all is still, you can see,
hear and know the truth that all is given.

Hence those moments when chaos seeks to destroy all you
have built, released, healed and are now
welcoming into your daily life experiences.

In these moments of Spiritual Expansion, it can often seem as
though you have been forsaken. This is not truth.

Seek once again the connection between mind, heart and Soul.

All is forgiven in the blink of an eye.

ANGEL LADY TERRIE MARIE, D.MS.

All is healed in the beating of a grateful, loving heart.

Accept that moment of seeming chaos. Bless it with love, releasing all as you exhale deeply creating space for that which is pure truth, light and love.

More awaits you. Allow yourself to recognize the present, is but a reflection of what once was. All comes to those who appear to wait, while in reality, they create space within through faith … persistent faith

CHAPTER THREE:
Are You Stepping into Your Value?

"Belief begins with faith ... stepping into Faith."

In so many ways, we tend to discount ourselves. Everyone, no matter how much money they have, love to save money and finding a bargain now and again. I'm the same way. When there are opportunities to save, I accept the fits and move on saying 'thank you' at my good fortune.

There's a HUGE difference between saving money and being cheap or tight-fisted with money. Here's what I mean ... if someone is always looking for the cheapest option, it is a reflection of what one truly feels about their worth and value. If you don't treat yourself to lunch out because you're always watching and counting every dollar, what you're really doing is treating your 'material supply' as limited instead of unlimited.

Now, a word of caution, this is not permission to spend without regard for what's necessary to cover financial obligations.

There have been times when I wondered how I was going to pay bills or when the next paying client or customer was going to show up. It is prudent to manage your financial resources wisely. It's also important to know WHEN to stretch out financially when opportunity presents itself.

One of the ways I gently, lovingly but very matter-of-factly 'state' to the Universe --- I'm not going to take this anymore – is to treat myself to lunch AND get dessert! This is a way to 'move' the energy blockage before it really gets lodged, requiring a jackhammer or explosives to clear your receiving channels.

If you're wondering what any of this has to do with stepping into your value, consider this ... if you're not willing to give yourself something nice every so often like:

* a bouquet of flowers
* going to the movies
* coffee with a friend
* taking a day away from everything
* a leisurely salt bath
* investing in yourself

What you're really telling the Universe, your Angels and your sub-conscious mind, is that you're not worthy or deserving of nice things OR attracting the right opportunities, clients and financial prosperity into your life and bank accounts.

Let's look at this from a different perspective ... if you don't wholly and completely believe that what you have to offer others through the lens of your unique life path experiences, you're 'saying' you're nothing special.

If you don't believe deep within that your experience and lessons learned, offer the potential for transformation, then why would anyone want to work with you or hire you to be their coach or mentor?

You've heard the saying "charity begins at home" ... right? Consider this well beautiful Soul, belief begins with faith ... stepping into Faith.

If you've ever felt disrespected and discouraged when sharing your deepest desires with someone --- and who hasn't! --- then chances are you have felt less than valuable. That old *stuff* said by someone or perhaps many someone's, stops you from fully stepping into your value.

It's like you dip your toes in the water and decide it's just too cold to go any further. So rather than 'dive-in' you pull back. It's the same fear based reaction when you attempt to step beyond the comfort zone even when you KNOW it's exactly what you need and probably asked for.

Each time you say 'no' you're really saying 'I'm not valuable, I don't deserve this (fill in the blank). And another layer of resistance is added, making it harder to get through the next time. For some people, there's so much negative resistance they just give up. I see it, hear it and feel it all the time from people who think they're doing something. In reality they are creating the illusion of taking action by saying they're going to do xyz when (something super specific happens or health gets better or ...).

If You Are Whispering Nobody Can Hear You or Your Message

Here's a case study of a guy name Bobby, a talented Tarot Reader ... before I became consciously aware of my connection with Angels, I had questions about my purpose for being here. LOTS of questions! The first Saturday of every month, the local metaphysical shop, Butterflies of Wisdom, held an open reading day for apprentice readers. Readings were given on a Love Offering basis.

One Saturday, I went to have my cards read. I REALLY needed insight. I liked Bobby's energy and asked him for a reading. He was spot on and it was the first of many steps to where I am today.

Several years later, Bobby came to one of the El Paso Psychic Fair events where I was a vendor selling crystals and giving Angelic Reiki sessions. He hadn't been giving readings for a few years for one reason or another … all of which he told me in detail! He began to ask me lots of questions about what to do next and how to go about getting a table at the fair. I answered his questions till customers were at my table.

Another couple of years passed and Bobby shows up again, asking the very same questions about how to get started. I repeated the answers and encouraged him to reach out to the organizers. I had a feeling he wouldn't, but I did my best to encourage him to take the next step.

Then one day, he found the courage and got a table at a local one-day event. It was poorly attended and Bobby didn't cover his table fee of $40. He felt incredibly disappointed and disillusioned and simply faded away confiding in me that it must not be what he came here to do. He just gave up after that one event.

The point is … the longer you wait to take that Leap into Faith, the more fear and doubt the conscious mind Ego-chitter chatter builds up resistance to you actually following your path and achieving the kind of success and fulfillment you dream about. Just sayin' …

No matter how gifted someone is, if they never take that next step, as scary as it almost always is, then they're just 'whispering' to themselves anyone else who will sort of listen about what they're going to do someday ... someday never ever becomes the present moment. Never!

Here's the other side of that ... if you're hiding out, afraid to let anyone know who you truly are, you're still in the 'Spiritual Closet.' There are so many beautiful Souls who are *terrified* to let anyone know why they are or what they dream of doing. That is very sad indeed. Please, do not let this be you. YOU have sooooo very much to offer!

You know, for a very long time, I was afraid of what people would say of think about me. For years, I really did my best to 'fit in' to be just like everyone else. And it was literally strangling my inner-Spirit. I was terrified of being different or thought of as a fraud.

Then on day, I made a decision to stop trying so damned hard to be like everybody else. It wasn't working and I was miserable. So I quit and started on an inner-journey I knew absolutely nothing about ... and it's just as well I didn't. If I did, I would have RUN in the other direction screaming "NO NO NO I'm NOT doing that it's just too hard!" Then I would have slammed the door shut, glued, taped and nailed it shut!

If you're not at least journaling about your purpose or your dreams of fulfilling that purpose, NO ONE will ever hear you or the message you came to share with others ... your inner-Spirit will forever remain silent.

It takes courage to take that first step and the next. It's not always easy. Sometimes it's downright hard and I've *'quit'* more times that I can count. Yes, here I am, many thousands upon thousands of steps later, sharing the journey with you, beautiful Soul.

Here's a special message for you from Uzzah, the Angel of Strength and Courage to help you when you need it most.

Angel Uzzah
Forever Your Champion

Beloved Child of Light, courage is deep within your heart and Soul every moment.

There is never one moment you do not have access to my brethren and me for support along your Earth journey path of fulfilling the very purpose for your being here in this present moment, in this present time.

This is a time of Great Awakening among the many.
It is your time now.

Be willing to breathe deeply,
exhaling all that stands in your way, past or present.

You are the only one who can reach deep within your Scared Heart Space.

You are the only one who can free you from the illusion of fear.

You are the only one who knows your true calling
in this place and time.

Trust the time is now for you to come forward
with strength and courage.

Call upon me and I shall be by your side
before the asking is complete.

True, your path has many pebbles, stones and at times,
boulders that require clearing.

Do not allow another to deter or distract you from your
deepest knowing of who you are and
what you came here to do.

I shall take your hand in mind.
Side by side we shall take the next step together.

I am forever your champion, beloved one.
Know this truth, lean on me now and in the moment of
your greatest need for strength and courage.

We are complete.

Are You Afraid to Be Seen?

When all of 'this' started more than 13 years ago, I was afraid, actually scared and frightened is more like it. I didn't want anyone to know I 'talked' to Angels and they 'talked' to me. Being completely transparent, it's been less than 12 months since making a super-conscious choice to come completely out of the *Spiritual Closet*. I believe there's always more 'out' within me especially as my vibration keeps going to the next higher level. Even so, at this moment, I have fully stepped into my value and am willing to be 'fully and completely seen'. Being willing to be 'seen' isn't easy and admittedly, there are times I feel like hiding out.

How do you know if you're hiding or not? Well, beautiful Soul, if you're afraid of what others are going to think or say about you … that's your first 'sign' that you're afraid to be 'seen.' To be clear, 'being seen' is not about putting you, your dreams or your beliefs *out there* for others to trample on or pooh-pooh as stupid, crazy or worse … so impossible *it'll never happen* no matter how hard or how long you work at it.

So how does one begin to stop hiding? You start with baby steps and lots of deep breaths. You make a decision to show-up for your dreams so you can begin to discover your true purpose for being here, now. What starts to happen next is quite magical, if you will allow it.

Everyone wants to know everything and every detail about their path and purpose. In truth, if we were given what we say we want, most of us (me included) would be paralyzed with fear of *HOW* it was ever going to manifest.

That's where Angels can truly help you clear the path, cut through illusion and show you the very next step that will then reveal the next step and the next.

You've probably heard this before --- we create our own reality and all we need to do is make a 'decision' and it becomes so. Well, don't know about you, but, I've made sooooo many decisions and then … nothing. I now understand that a 'decision' without conviction deep within and determined persistence, has little to no value. If there's *no deep-seated belief energy*, *then absolutely nothing happens* that helps you move forward to creating a new or better reality.

The first and most important person that MUST absolutely

believe in you and your dreams is you. If you don't absolutely beyond a shadow of a doubt believe, anyone and can come along to derail you because they project their fears, jealousy or envy onto you and your dreams. So not only do you have our own *stuff* to get through, now you have their *stuff* to get through too.

It boils down to these two essential ingredients … self-esteem and having a sense of being empowered. You are the one person who giveth and taketh away from you. Zuphlas is the Angel of Self-Esteem and Empowerment. Call upon him to help you find and tap into these two essential ingredients that will help you move forward every step of the way.

Angel Zuphlas
Belief Beyond Reason

In your path you must believe all is shown to you
in its full completeness.

Upon acceptance of this truth, all is given in time and
true measure of your readiness beloved one.

No thing, person or experience presenting itself as opportunity,
shall be denied you.

It is you who must do the choosing at times,
moment by moment, step by step, breath by breath.

In those moments of complete and utter acceptance,
all is laid at your feet.

Belief beyond reason simply requires your complete surrender

of doubt, fear and of all naysayers including that which resides within your thoughts and emotions.
Belief beyond reason is rooted in faith.

Have faith that you are indeed guided with only the highest of intentions and matching vibrations.

When all is aligned, the magic of all Creation is laid before you for the taking, giving and receiving.

You have a belief beyond reason or you do not. It is simple. It is clear.

Choice is laid upon your heart.

Which do you choose?

CHAPTER FOUR:
Fear Freezes All Your Assets

"Do you allow fear to stop you from taking that Leap into Faith?"

Fear is the single most destructive culprit of your dreams, goals and aspirations for a better life and living your purpose full-out and all-in.

In this instance, your assets are ...

- your deepest desires of a better life for you and your family
- being able to manifest what you need and want, enabling you to fulfill your purpose
- the on-demand ability to connect with your inner-intuitive self and your Angels
- your gift of being able to stand your ground, stepping into your value fully and completely
- the ability of tapping into guidance with confidence, trust and faith

- being able to see clearly, the unfolding of your path as it reveals itself and the next best step
- belief in the vision you've been given and the strength, courage, determination and persistent commitment to fulfill that vision

The conscious mind feeds and breeds fear and doubt. Illusion is the ultimate deception that you are not worthy or deserving of charging for your time, energy and above all, for your gifts. You have been given specific gifts to accomplish the very purpose of your existence here and now in physical form.

The notion that to be *Spiritual* is to "not want" is one of the most insidious tricks of those who would see you fail at any cost. To be of service is at the forefront of every Light Worker's heart, thoughts and intentions. What the conscious mind Ego-chitter chatter fails to concede, is that being of service, is about being of service first to you.

Said differently, to be of service, is to nurture the Self so one does not deplete their energy to such drastic levels as to be non-existent. It is a gross dis-service to place all others before the Self without regard for the care-taking of one's energy and connection to Spirit itself.

Fear holds you in a space of limitation and lack because of what others may say or think about you. There will always be those who choose to focus outside of themselves, avoiding lack and limitation in their lives. People, most people, choose the way of not focusing on themselves as a means of feeling better about what is not happening in their own lives, relationships, careers and businesses.

For some, it is safer to remain in the shadows of what could be rather than risk failure. Success is in the doing, taking each step as it is revealed along the path of fulfilling your purpose.

Fear freezes your assets, which also freezes your dreams until they wither into the dark abyss of nothingness. That is all there is. There is nothing more to be said on this matter. We now move forward to the next of realization.

Does Fear Drive You into Submission or Propel You Forward?

We, all of us, begin our lives with tales of not talking to strangers and speaking aloud. Fear is the conscious mind's control mechanism, whose sole purpose is to keep you safe from making a fool of yourself. it, fear, through conscious mind Ego-chitter chatter, will lie to you. It will cheat you out of your dreams if you allow it.

When things are going well for you, have you noticed that *something happens*? A memory will come up that brings up a painful experience. Maybe something happens to someone in your family or to a close friend and somehow you're the one person who *has* to handle it. Believe it or not, this a way the conscious mind has of controlling just how much good comes into your life.

Do you allow fear to stop you from taking that Leap into Faith and going for it OR do you take a deep breath and do it anyway? Some use fear as a sign they are about to do something outside of their comfort-zone. I've heard people many people say they use fear in a positive way, like proving to someone or to themselves that they are not a loser. Whatever the motivation, fear can and often does paralyze most people even if it is only for a few moments. Fear is the root of procrastination or perfectionism. Either one creates 'wait energy' which becomes heavy negative energy.

Negativity in any form holds you, your dreams and your

purpose hostage. Pure and simple, fear feeds doubt. Doubt grows fear. Fear becomes an incapacitating, all consuming monster, preventing your light to shine. Let me tell you 'bout fear ... nah, nah, nah ... let me tell you the story of how I left the Light IN after the darkness threatened to silence me forever.

When your computer dies and takes everything --- 5 ½ years of work and channeling --- with it, it feels like the entire Universe is against you and even the Angels have abandoned you. Surely, it must be a sign you've *F*** up royally! When you are going in the wrong direction and you keep ignoring the signs ... all of them ... something drastic is bound to happen that will free you to pay attention. The lessons can be soft or extreme. There is always a choice. It's okay to make course corrections or tweak a message.

You can choose to be pummeled into submission or use fear as a stepping stone to get to the next level of vibration, or take your career or business to that level of success and prosperity. Fear can be paralyzing if you allow it to consume your thoughts, actions and emotions.

Should you find yourself beginning to go down a path you don't want to go down, call upon Nathaniel, the Angel of Fire and Energy Purification. This all-powerful Angel of Fire will help you release yourself from the grip of fear, the conscious mind Ego-chitter chatter would have you believe is real.

ANGELS SUCCESS AND PROSPERITY

Angel Nathaniel
Fear Is An Illusion

Fear is a means of hiding behind the mask others have
cast upon you.

Do not allow another to create a mask to hide behind.

Do not allow the mask to color your breath,
your steps upon the path before you.

Bring all to me for cleansing from within, to the surface to be
burned from you in Spiritual Fires of purifying Soul and heart.

Breathe in the Light of a thousand white candles.
Breathe out all that does not serve your highest and best good,
Child of Light.

As the burning off all that is not of love and light begins,
be at peace with that which is, in this moment.

The clearing must be complete before the
unfolding begins in earnest.

See fear as a frightened child alone in the dark.

As the Light approaches, shadows fall away, bathed in love
with grace and compassion. Choosing instead to see fear as a
signpost of growth and expansion along your journey of
achieving all that has been shown to you.

You are blessed beyond your knowing,
beyond your current level of understanding.

If you will but place one foot upon the path before you,
one after the other, you will begin to see more clearly each day.

Trust is the essential key to unlocking all that is already yours.

Be at peace. Be at peace now and for all your days.

How Fear Scams You into Giving Up

We've talked about how *fear* is a deceitful trickster full of treachery at every turn. It will be the biggest challenge on your journey as a Spiritual Being having a human experience. It will distract you from the truth as often as possible.

The sole purpose, from the viewpoint of conscious mind Ego-chitter chatter, is to keep you in the *zone of comfort*, where failure, failure, ridicule and the cruelty of others is non-existent. The *zone of comfort* is pure illusion because there will always be those who's tongues will wag, taking the spotlight off themselves to shine elsewhere.

Take this as a sign you are creating a powerful impact within your life and in the lives of those around you. If this were not a truth, there would be nothing negative given or projected in your direction. The projection of condemnation, ridicule, judgment and criticism as a positive sign you are walking your path the way it was intended.

Fear creates boundaries to stay within, woven with lack and limitation no matter the desires of your heart of dreams given to you. It will con you into giving up on yourself, accepting the stories of others --- well-meaning or not --- as your truth. A statement, repeated often enough, becomes a belief. A belief practiced long enough, becomes a truth. Always remember, a false, fear-based truth can be dissolved and re-programmed with or struggle. The choice, the beautiful Soul, is always yours to make.

If you choose to give-up on knowing your purpose, you condemn yourself and all you came here to do, to remain an illusion and in the shadows of *the greatest scammer of all* ... fear.

Do not, or ever, allow your sweet voice to be silenced for fear of what others will say or think of you. Do not allow conscious mind Ego-chitter chatter to dictate your level of success and prosperity ... ever!

Ask Chairoum, the Angel of Clearing Illusion from Your Path to help you discern truth from illusion.

Angel Chairoum
Clearing Illusion from Your Path

When you, beloved child, are in the midst of the forest of your
countless thoughts, emotions become muddled,
dark and dingy.

Taking the next step along the path before you is necessary to
breathe life into that which is deep within your heart space.

See all that attempts to block your natural energy flow for fear
of being seen, as beautiful rounded stone steps to place your
feet upon.

ANGEL LADY TERRIE MARIE, D.MS.

Being willing to be willing to see the truth among the many thoughts of distraction, is a gift given to you, through the Light of the Divine and that of my brethren and I.

We are ever near to aid you upon your path.
You need only ask to be bathed in the Light, body and Soul.

Illusion is an all-consuming fear of failure.

Illusion is the unnatural death of your deepest desires and that of your purpose being fulfilled wholly and completely.

It is in the letting go of fear based thoughts, emotions smooth through love of Self, illuminating the way before you.

As you clear your mind, beloved one,
you begin to see all more clearly.

In the Light, there is no darkness,
nothing hides from the Light.

In the Light, there is clarity.

In the Light, there is peace and harmony.

In the Light, insights are clearly given.

In the Light, is all you seek.

CHAPTER FIVE:
What Is Your True Reality Really?

"It is the silence that all is given to you."

The truth of your reality is what you see manifesting around you, right now, this moment, beautiful Soul. It is also truth that your current reality is a reflection of the past, your past. All you have ever thought, felt, said and done has brought you to this moment, in the here and now.

As you read these pages, there is a seamless flow from one chapter to the next. Even though there has been a 120 day hiatus, as I have experienced many shifts in energy and consciousness. Allow me to explain …

At the beginning of 2017, I launched a brand new, comprehensive Mentoring Certification Program. I was really excited and scared too. This program was the culmination of 7+ years of teaching, mentoring, learning, expansion and personal growth. And, it was the next piece of the overall vision given to me through a trusted friend and the Angels themselves, many, many years ago.

There were four people who said 'yes' and I was really looking forward to sharing the journey with these amazing women! Then all of a sudden, two women backed out. Okay, I said to myself, taking a VERY deep breath and letting go at the same time. But that wasn't the end of things. Another person chose to quit after just 30 days. Still, I honored the commitment and for the next 6 months, I worked with the one remaining woman who stuck with her commitment. And the transformation she experienced each step of the way, was truly phenomenal!

What I didn't fully comprehend until just a few days ago, was how that set of actions rocked my self-confidence mojo. There were a few more contributing factors, like my owing more for 2016 taxes than planned, which compounded the lower self-confidence. I was just making ends meet for the next five months. Talk about really being out over the edge of everything! I was frustrated, angry, disappointed and felt like my beloved Angels' were not really supporting me to the best of their capability.

They were and always are doing all they can. If I knowingly or unknowingly allow myself to be triggered by circumstances beyond my control … there's little the Angels can do to override the trigger until it has been fully recognized, healed and released.

We do indeed create our own reality and it is up to each one of us to do whatever it takes to get to that 'thing' the 'Blind Spot' that keeps us stuck where we don't want to be.

Your Inner-Game VS Fear = Manifestation

There's a lot of talk about the Inner-Game and how it controls what we see, hear and manifestation in our physical world. The control mechanism is the conscious mind. For the most part, the conscious mind just rambles on-and-on, mostly nonsense because it has one purpose and one purpose only --- to keep you in your place of fear and doubt.

I remember when I just learned about meditation and what it could mean for my Spiritual Growth and all I had to do was sit still and be quiet for 20 minutes every day. Well! Sitting still was not and for the most part, still is NOT part of vocabulary! It was one of the most difficult and challenging things I ever attempted. After many years of practicing meditation, it has become some of my most treasured moments of my day.

It is in the silence that all is given to us like guidance, answers and clarity about the next steps along our respective paths. When I am able to quiet the conscious mind Ego-chitter chatter, I find that zone of peacefulness. In the silence between breaths, there is expansion. A sense of utter knowing all is indeed well and in Divine Order.

In those moments, all I truly desire is in alignment, on all levels of vibration --- emotionally, mentally, energetically and Spiritually. Being in the "zone of knowing" is pure heaven for me. In the "zone" time is stretched with grace and ease, messages and guidance from my beloved Angel companions are continuous and loving.

This is the 'space' where my Inner-Game is completely in-tune with my path, enabling me to fulfill the purpose for which I came to be here now, doing what I am doing.

Whatever thoughts and emotions are dominant ... those occupying the most 'space' in your heart and conscious mind, is what manifest physically in your life and work. If you're not completely convinced of this beautiful Soul, take a look around at what is showing up for you OR not showing up for you. If you are not where you want to be --- OR --- well on your way, you're not yet fully aware of how your thoughts and emotions are in total control of all you are experiencing in the here and now.

As you choose to become more consciously aware of all you say and do and how what you don't want is showing itself to you, you are then able to begin changing how you see your current reality.

Fear is a primary driving force in the lives of countless people world-wide. People fear making a wrong decision or going down the wrong path, so they choose nothing and end up doing nothing at all. More choices are made through the lens of fear and doubt than through love and fear.

Fear creates more fear. Doubt creates more doubt. Fear and doubt manifest more of the same. It truly is a vicious cycle unless and until you make a conscious decision to get off the proverbial merry-go-round, tapping into your Inner-Self and the Angels themselves.

Each moment gifts you with the gift of choosing something different ... a new thought and a new way to feel your way forward, step-by-step to where you truly desire to be, do and have.

Archangel Uriel is the Angel whose primary mission is to help each and every one of us manifest our truest desires, the desires that rise from the depths of your Soul. Be open to all that Archangel Uriel shares with you in his message.

ANGELS SUCCESS AND PROSPERITY

Archangel Uriel
Release the Outcome

Every moment is a manifestation of your thoughts
the energy of that which you feel.

Every emotion feeds your thoughts. Every thought feeds your thoughts. Every thought, in turn feeds your emotions.

Thoughts and emotions are what determine the quality of all that manifests physically in each moment.

Many feel as though they lack the ability of manifesting their desires, when in truth, you are all master manifestors.

Thoughts determine things in not a new concept yet it remains. So many among you do not yet fully comprehend it's meaning in full measure.

In those moments of complete trust, all falls into place for your highest and best good and for the good of all concerned.

Yet many place their energetic focus on the exact opposite of all they truly desire. This is not the way, beloved child of love and light to attain that which you desire most in this life.

The way is through the releasing of the outcome,
most often measured in time and quantity rather than allowing the fullness of all you desire to manifest in its highest and most powerful form.

Become more aware of what you feel.
Become more aware of the litany of thoughts you allow to flow through your conscious mind.

Be mindful of what you see and how you say things.

Remember, beloved one, all manifests without judgement as to lack or abundance.

We are complete in this moment.

What Does Your Inner-Game Really Manifest into Your Life?

Have you ever heard someone say something like --- "I'm really a positive person." --- And then the very next thing out of their mouth is a complaint? Most people are not fully aware of their thoughts and the things they say. Ours, unfortunately, is primarily a negative based society. It's as if there's a mandate to find fault with anyone or anything that is different.

Negativity in any form breeds, attracts and manifests more of the same. It is the Law of Attraction at its best. Energy is everything and everything is energy. There is no way round this. So beautiful Soul, stop and ask yourself what kinds of thoughts are going round and round in your beautiful head?

What *stories* are you telling yourself as to why you have not yet manifested the vision of fulfilling your purpose? These stories, while they placate the humanness of your being, are illusions getting in the way of actually allowing all you desire to manifest through you with grace and ease.

When you are at peace, feeling and being content, many things and opportunities simply *appear as if out of thin air*. In essence, this is truth and is also a clear demonstration of the Law of Attraction in action. The Angels and the Universe are always conspiring in your favor. Yet ... there are so many different layers of resistance that have been created and reinforced through your current life-time. Resistance shows itself in obvious and not so obvious ways.

Whatever you choose to believe, know this above all else ... you are, always have and always will be a master manifestor. If you don't like or want what continues to show itself to you, then change your inward focus. Become aware of your thoughts. If you must, record your thoughts for the next 48 hours. What is the predominant theme? Are there more complaints or happy, positive thoughts?

Next become keenly aware of what you say to yourself and to others. This is the key to changing what kinds of things, people and situations you are currently attracting into your life, relationships, work and business.

The more consciously aware you truly are, beautiful Soul, the more you will be able to create new pathways from the conscious mind to the sub-conscious mind. The sub-conscious mind is a kind of 'dumping ground' of all thoughts and emotions. It does not discern or judge between positive and negative. It literally absorbs everything.

If you are not where you want to be, doing what you want to be doing, be willing to go within. Thoughts do determine the having and the not having. It is that simple and that complex all in the same moment.

Your Inner-Game controls what does and does not manifest for you. Here's a case study that really gives you an inside-look at just how powerful the Inner-Game really is ...

Case Study: How Stephanie Freed Herself from a Poverty Mindset

Allow me to introduce you to Stephanie. She is an amazing, intuitive, Spiritual woman, owns her own business and has been blessed with a special gift of being able to help others see what's really blocking them from getting what they truly want and desire to manifest in their lives.

The challenge for this beautiful woman has been not being to get to the bottom, her unique 'Blind Spot'... that memory that set her up for a lifetime of struggling and hardship. Stephanie hired me to help her get her B.S. out of the way. She had managed to get quite a bit cleared out on her own, but, like so many on their Spiritual Clean-Up Path ™, she didn't know what was holding her back from really moving forward with her business and having a consistent stream of financial prosperity.

At first she didn't really understand WHY it was necessary to clean-up conscious mind Ego-chitter chatter because all she really wanted to do was get to the bottom line and fix it. During her first session, she began to realize that there was sooooo much 'stuff' free-floating in her thoughts; it was creating a kind-of bottle-neck in her emotions which kept feeding her thoughts which in turn created her energy flow to be sluggish and get bogged down.

After a few sessions and taking action --- implementing the Action Steps --- a memory that had been buried sooooo deeply, Stephanie didn't even remember it was there! We're talking something that had happened when she was 13 or 14 years old!

This ONE experience had been impacting her life for nearly 50 YEARS!

ANGELS SUCCESS AND PROSPERITY

Stephanie has given me permission to share this with you ... she had been invited to the Spring Cotillion by a boy she liked who was attending a Military Academy in Virginia. Stephanie was soooo excited and images of the magical night were dancing in her mind. She had a regular babysitting gig every Friday night and her parents forbid

Stephanie from asking for the night off. She could go to the Cotillion ONLY if her babysitting clients canceled on their own without her telling them anything.

Well, Stephanie didn't get to do to the Cotillion and she had to write to this boy and tell she couldn't go. To say that this crushed her is an understatement.

Fast forward and she was still holding herself to the decision she made ... you see, her parents were trying to teach her about honoring her commitments. The *MESSAGE* Stephanie HEARD was the *EXACT OPPOSITE*. She made this 'story' in her head about always having to sacrifice her dreams for someone else and that she had to work EXTRA HARD to FINALLY get what she wanted.

We did some *DEEP HEALING* work and Stephanie began to not only *FEEL* differently, she began to *SEE* results the very next day! She knows there's a bit more to do but she is *NOW FREE* from that memory that had been buried so deeply she hadn't even remembered it.

When you're ready, ask Asaph, the Angel of the Written Word, to help you become more in-tune with the words you use as you write out your deepest desires as if there are no limits place upon you.

ANGEL LADY TERRIE MARIE, D.MS.

Angel Asaph
Clear Intention

Speak as though there is instant manifestation, Dear One.

For in truth there is. It is called vibration,
found in the tone of your words and
the depths of your emotions.

See clearly all you desire.
Yes, this you have done countless times.

Now, choose to see differently.

Choose to see through a clear heart as if there is nothing and
no one standing in between where you are and
where you truly desire to be.

All is made whole in the asking.
All is made manifest in the receiving.
Clear your mind. Clear your heart. Clear your inner vision of
all you have seen, knowing you are free to simply and
completely be whole and complete.

When the mind is clear of all negative debris,
the way is also made clear.

Trust this is so beloved one and you shall begin to see more of
all you truly desire, come to life as if by *magic*!

It is only *magic* to those who do not see what you have chosen
to release in the setting of clear intention.

ANGELS SUCCESS AND PROSPERITY

Know this is so.

All is made manifest in the allowing through clear intention.

We are now complete on this matter.

CHAPTER SIX:
What's Next?

"Change begins first with a deep heart-felt desire."

Such a simple, straight forward question and yet it can literally cause you to freeze-up. It has done that to me many, many times! It's easy to *see* the vision of fulfilling our Life Purpose. I still remember the first glimpse of exactly what the Angels have shown me and others close to me. The stumbling block is getting from where you are, to where you want to be.

Not being able to visualize the path even a little of how puts a sense of *panic* in the conscious mind and here's why. The conscious mind, your conscious mind only has past experiences and the beliefs you have inherited from previous generations to draw upon as real possibilities for you to manifest, achieve and accomplish in this life.

You see beautiful Soul; there is reference point for something you haven't yet experienced. This is where vision boards and visualizing can help you minimize the amount of *time* we feel is required and eliminate obstacles to manifesting your dreams.

When was the last time you really took your dreams out and dusted them off? I don't mean the last time you *thought* about it or *wished* your dream was already a reality. If it's been several months, then take some time and look … *really look* at your vision board or what you've written out. You're not the same person you were when you first created your vision board or wrote out it looks and feels like to be living your dreams of fulfilling your purpose full-out and all-in … with a no-holds-barred approach.

Every if your dream is mostly the same, there are parts and pieces that no longer fit. There are, more than likely, new pieces of your vision that have been revealed to you along the way. It's not time to release the parts and pieces that no longer resonate, keeping what does resonate and create space for the updated parts and pieces.

What's next is being able to let go of what others (family, friends and colleagues) think you should or shouldn't do.

What's next is coming out from behind the mask you've been wearing for fear of what others might say of think about you.

What's next is getting really real with you about what you desire, deep within your heart center.

What's next is taking a deep breath stepping out to the edge of everything you have ever known and *Stepping into Faith*, knowing there will be stones to step upon or you'll be given wings to fly!

What's next is … believing in you, your dreams and your path will reveal itself to you in amazingly magical and mystical ways!

What If You Could?

Seriously beautiful Soul ... what if you really could pull this off? How fabulously fulfilling would that be for you? Think about it. Really ... just think about it.

Knowing what's below the surface, holding you and your dreams hostage just disappears as if by magic, is your Golden Ticket to living the life you're destine to live. And all you have to do is get out of the way! Imagine stepping out of the shadows of negative self-talk, beliefs, fear and doubt and into the Light of who you truly are!

We, the Angels and I, already see you --- *yes YOU beautiful Soul YOU* --- living the life you've barely given yourself permission to see fully for fear of never being able to have the vision you've seen and been given come to life.

So many beautiful Souls' just like you, or someone you know have been taught to pursue the *safe path* and to 'fit in' at any cost. I used to be on *that path of fitting in* at all costs. It was killing my Spirit and my Light was barely a flickering flame. Then one day, I made a decision to stop the craziness that was killing me softly, and get off that never-ending merry-go-round. It was the scariest, most rewarding, freeing decision ever!

In truth, had I known how challenging it would be, we would not be having this conversation. And, being open and completely transparent with you ... there have been countless moments I quit! Yes, deep down, below the hurt, frustration and disillusion, there is always *a knowing* that the Dark Night of the Soul passed, I would begin again.

Each time there is a releasing and letting go of the old, space is created for that which is being revealed to you.

Take the writing and channeling of this book for example. It's nearly 12 months since the idea was given to me during meditation. There have been obstacles like having misplaced my self-confidence mojo and discovering 'Blind Spots' that had been buried under years of hiding behind fear of being *seen*.

What if you could do this too ... tap into intuition and your Angels, along your unique, magical and mystical path to fulfilling your purpose, living the life you're destined to live in Light, Love and complete contentment?

Haziel, the Angel of Vision, will help you *see beyond* your current reality and tap into your unlimited potential.

Angel Haziel
Seeing This Moment and Beyond Clearly

Dear Beloved Child of Light and Love, you are so much more than you allow yourself to know.

You are more than you have been allowed to believe.
Till now.

Begin by being willing to be willing to see into the depth of your Soul. Be willing to see all that is before you with open eyes, open mind and willing heart.

Close your eyes beloved one, be willing to journey the path before you with grace, love and compassion.

The path chosen is not for the faint of heart. The path chosen is not for those content to remain in the shadows of their fears.

Be at peace with all the shadows those who have gone before you. Be at peace knowing you now create your path walking more fully in the Light.

Allow all that has come before this very moment, to slip away from sight. Allow your most Sacred Dreams to see the Light with love, healing, fully manifested.

Allow you to accept the many gifts given along the way, trusting you are indeed closer to fulfilling your purpose.

Transformation from the Inside Out is Crucial to Your Ultimate Success and Prosperity

Change begins first with a deep heart-felt desire, followed by the decision to commit to doing whatever it takes to accomplish the letting go of all that no longer resonates within, and perhaps did. Determination to face one's inner-demons is the next piece that must then slip into place both consciously and emotionally.

The battle then begins in earnest. Conscious-mind Ego-chitter chatter raises the volume and intensity of its barrage of fear of losing control. It is at this point, most give-up, settling back into the familiar patterns of thought and emotion. Each time you choose to take a step backwards, it becomes increasingly difficult to move through the layers of resistance that have been created and reinforced along the way.

In fairness, we remind you that some barriers have been inherited through the very DNA that flows within and through your physical body and reinforced during your childhood days. These barriers have, more than likely, also been reinforced throughout your life to this day. This is not permission to throw your hands up in the air disavowing all responsibility for all that has and has not happened in your life. It is now the time to relinquish control, surrendering all that is not yours to carry.

In the letting go, there is alignment with your purpose and a re-alignment with your Soul Essence, the truth of who you are. As hurt and disappointment give way to forgiveness, healing begins at the deepest levels of consciousness, creating a new pattern reaching into the depths of the sub-conscious-mind. It is here --- the sub-conscious-mind --- that true healing begins with unconditional love and the willingness to forgive others for all the many wrongs done unto you and by you unto others.

It is essential to forgive oneself for having participated in any wrong-doing that caused another pain. Forgiving the Self is also about recognizing and releasing you from all that has ever been said to you or about you, causing you to no longer believe in yourself. People say and do hurtful, less than loving things to cause another pain, which, in the moment, elevates themselves through anger and hate.

Forgiveness is no longer exchanging negative energy with another on any level. It frees you to move about your life without carrying the burdens of hurt, disappointment, heartbreak and betrayal. As long as one continues to carry the burdens of the past within their heart and mind, one is forever imprisoned in hurt, shame and possible even guilt about their own actions. It is that simple and complex all in the same moment beloved one.

Change begins first with a desire. As the caterpillar goes within, so must you, to truly experience an ever-lasting transformation from the inside out. Or risk remaining in the shadows of your true self, never really stepping more fully into the Light with each step. There is always a time of transition. This is often referred to as a Dark Night of the Soul or an inner-journey of deep self-reflection. During this in-betweeness or transition, your faith and your beliefs will be challenged to the very core of your being and understanding. Nothing will 'fit' as space is being created deep within for the ultimate transformation.

Then one day, the skies will begin to clear and the Light will be clearer and brighter than ever before as a new path is revealed to you. You must start at once, taking even one or two small steps to ensure all you have faced does not re-insert itself in your heart and mind.

The person you are in this moment *will not* get you or allow you to step up to the next level of vibration, success or prosperity you desire to achieve and experience.

For there to permanent changes on the outside, in your life, work, business and relationships, there must first be change on the inside. This is indeed the one and only pathway to clearing the way for all you truly desire deep within your heart.

Choose one thing, one experience or less-than-happy memory to start. Allow you to fully embrace the hurt and the joy, turning to embrace the whole. Only then, beautiful Soul, will you fully heal both heart and mind, freeing the natural flow of your energy in every area of your life. Allow Ezekiel, the Angel of Transformation to guide you now ...

Angel Ezekiel
Transcend the Past, Freeing Your Future

All begins within Beloved Child of Love and Light.
All is held in bitterness or in love.

Choose wisely as each choice then builds upon the other as stepping stones beyond what you now know to be your truth.

Call upon me to assist you in building stepping stones of love and healing rather than fear and hate.

The seeds you plant in this moment and in the next are what you shall harvest in the days yet to come.

As you empty what is now behind you from your heart, your mind, you create space deep within for new, more loving energy with which to fertilize you dreams of fulfilling your purpose the way it is intended.

There is always a choice of how to live your purpose or abandon it all together.

No matter the choices made, you are loved beyond measure now and always. Know this truth to be so for all your days.

Call upon me, I will help you each step of the way, by your side, without fail. Without judgement.
Without condemnation.

This is my gift to you now and always.

Next Steps ...

As you begin this next chapter of your journey, I'm available to assist you if you

- Are interested in getting your B.S story out the way, experiencing massive mindset shifts so that you can re-program the conscious-mind into becoming your ally instead of disrupting your flow at every turn
- Connect to your Inner-Intuitive Self and your Angels for clear answers, guidance and messages that will help you trust you are making the right and perfect choices and decisions for you, your purpose and your path
- Need help figuring out what the bottom line 'Blind Spot' is that keeps tripping you up, triggering feelings of not being worthy or deserving of having the success and prosperity you want and know is possible, if you just knew how
- Want to create the kind of 24/7 relationship with your Angels, or Spirit Guides, to know they are always with you and how to easily recognize and understand what you're getting, trusting all you're getting ... even the messages and signs you're missing right now

- Are ready to take your intuitive skills, gifts and abilities to the next level enabling you to raise your vibration to the next level and beyond as you begin to fulfill your Life Purpose in ways that work for you so you can help your clients get to their next level of vibration and, in turn fulfill their purpose full-out and all-in

YOU are special. *YOU* are unique. *YOUR* message and *YOUR* voice are needed *NOW* more than ever. It is *YOUR* turn to *SHINE* more brightly than ever before, taking your dreams, goals and desires to the next level with confidence and the tools that will help you not only get there, but stay at that next and the next ... the stars are there for you to soar beyond ... the only limits are those we place on ourselves.

Much love, Light, Peace and Purpose,
The Angel Lady Terrie Marie, D.Ms.

Let's connect beautiful Soul!

Email: TerrieMarie@AngelDreamTeam.com
Twitter: https://twitter.com/angelladytm (use the phrase, I'm ready to become a mover & shaker of my reality)
Facebook: https://www.facebook.com/AngelDreamTeam/
Instagram: https://www.instagram.com/angelladytm/

To connect with the Angel Lady Terrie Marie, and receive a Free Gift, visit her website at:
http://www.angeldreamteam.com/

What if you could share what you do and who you help in a way that people respond, "YES!" excited to work with you?

Hi, I'm Michelle Shaeffer. **I show entrepreneurs just like you how to share their businesses in a way that attracts perfect-fit clients.**

As a blogger, speaker, marketing consultant and human psychology junkie… who also happens to be just a little bit "woo woo"… **I understand you, I see the amazing value you offer,** and I can help you take what you do, and translate it from heavenly spiritual terms into real-world language that your ideal clients will understand.

I'd like to give you free access to a special video training series that will show you step by step how to easily and quickly:

➡ **Get inside your ideal client's head** so you understand how you can relate what you offer to the problems they want to fix (**so more of them say YES** to hiring you).

➡ Identify what pieces of your life story, your background, your experience, and **your gifts make you stand out and allow you to shine, attracting people to you easily.**

➡ Create a short "pitch" that zeroes in like a laser on exactly who you help, how you help them, and why -- in a way that **feels GREAT to share AND gets an immediate "Wow! Tell me more!"** from your listeners.

➡ Plus more… to give you **a solid marketing foundation in your business that's in alignment with who you are and your values** - no sleazy, scammy, icky marketing here - just honest, passionate ways to share how you serve so you can grow your business and make a difference in the world

To get FREE access to this video series, just go to www.michelleshaeffer.com/angels

A Gift for You From

Claim Your Life Consultant Course with Certification

Help others know what they want out of life and Know what they value

Answer the Call Today!
http://bit.ly/2gfRxuX

Boni Oian

830-537-4523

Boni@ClaimYourLifewithBoni.com

Are you ready to make a powerful impact every time you talk confidently about the amazing transformation you provide your clients and customers?

Marjorie Saulson
Speaking & Marketing Mentor
Top Speaking Coach of the Year

Have fears or discomfort tripped you up when you try to:

Network?   Answer questions in a meeting?
Talk on the phone?   Appear on a podcast, radio or TV?
Speak from the stage? Speak to someone about your business?

Then it's time to discover 10 Powerful Pathways to Overcome Your Public Speaking Fears (even if you have struggled with them for years)

This step-by-step report can guide you to confident, enthusiastic presentations that make all the difference

**Get your free report here
OvercomeYourSpeakingFears.com**

ANGELS SUCCESS AND PROSPERITY

Ready to begin Manifesting YOUR Magic!!

Hey there soul sister! I see you. I feel your light. You are a spiritual seeker looking to know your Soul, your gifts and life purpose in a deeper way.

You know there is more to you than your physical body. You are a soul in a body, having a human experience, on this planet, at this time. You want more for yourself and your magical life. You desire to create an abundant life in all areas. You want to enhance your spiritual gifts. You want to move past all the "stuff" holding you back from being your most magical self.

Working with Caroline will:

*help you learn who you truly are at Soul level

*help you discover your unique gifts and talents

*help you learn how you best manifest your goals

*help you release the energetic blocks (beliefs, thoughts, past life traumas, etc) that are holding you back and keeping you stuck

Caroline is a healer helping women who are confused about their life purpose, embrace their gifts so they can make more money, have meaningful relationships and enjoy vibrant health!

She can be found at **www.carolinenixon.net**.

Here is a **FREE** gift of energy healing to help you release stuck energy so you can embrace all that you ARE!

https://apowerfulhealingforyou.gr8.com

ANGEL LADY TERRIE MARIE, D.MS.

OTHER PRODUCTS
by Angel Lady Terrie Marie, D.Ms.

BOOKS

Sacred Angel Realms: A Coloring Journal
365 Daily Angel Messages: from Your Angels for Healing, Inspiration and Guidance
Inner-Balance and Harmony: Angel Messages Mediation Journal
https://www.amazon.com/Terrie-Marie/e/B00ALBRVBY/

AUDIO PROGRAMS and MEDITATION CDs

Manifest with Angels 2.0: Focus Your Intentions
Earth Mother to Sky Father Chakra Alignment
Connecting with Angels: How to Receive Guidance and Messages from Angels
You, Your Energy and Money! The Friendly Side of Money

SELF-STUDY COURSES

Guardian Angels On Call: How to Create Your Personal 24/7 Relationship
Divine Magic: Nine Sacred Secrets to Divine Wealth
How to Create Your Ultimate Angel Dream Team

ANGELS SUCCESS AND PROSPERITY

MISCELLANEOUS

Wings of Spirit Angel Cards (44 card-set)
Love and Romance Angel Cards (5 card-set)
Chakra Angel Cards (9 card-set)
Archangel Cards (5 card-set)

All of the above may be ordered by visiting:
http://www.angeldreamteam.com/
or through Angel Lady Terrie Marie, D. Ms. At
TerrieMarie@AngelDreamTeam.com

ANGEL LADY TERRIE MARIE, D.MS.

Connect with the Angel Lady Terrie Marie, D.Ms.

ANGEL DREAM TEAM
http://www.angeldreamteam.com/

FREE REPORT: SPECIAL WHITE PAPER REPORT
Angels Success and Prosperity: Become a Mover and Shaker of Your Reality: http://www.angeldreamteam.com/

BLOG
http://www.angeldreamteam.com/blog

FACEBOOK
https://www.facebook.com/AngelDreamTeam/

YOUTUBE
https://www.youtube.com/channel/UC2TOHSWJ53K4fDD_bM9H-xg

TWITTER
https://twitter.com/AngelLadyTM

INSTAGRAM
https://www.instagram.com/angelladytm/

About The Angel Lady Terrie Marie, D.Ms.

"Until you are fully aligned, you are not fully expressed. And when you are in alignment, things happen with the speed of Angels Wings."

The Angel Lady Terrie Marie's sole purpose is to guide Spiritual Growth Seekers, Healers, Readers and Spiritual Entrepreneurs worldwide to become movers and shakers of their realities in as few as 90 days.

After as little as one session, her clients have immediately booked more business, closed more sales, dramatically increased their cash flow and even earned career promotions in less than 3 days.

Still others reported feeling less stressed, more at peace, making better decisions faster, enjoying being engaged in regular Spiritual practices, and even manifesting significant financial windfalls to pay for life's little pleasures or new business undertakings.

This highly-gifted intuitive inspires clients to reach for and achieve their full potential. She teaches her students to connect to

Angels in ways that work for them. This creates clarity of mind, heart and Soul.

Messages channeled directly from Angels go beyond the prophetic. They provide, practical information that inspires clients to take massive action, becoming movers and shakers of their reality.

As clients recognize and receive the guidance and messages they want and need, they raise their inner-vibration. They experience massive mindset shifts. Best of all, they attract more opportunities, better clients, and financial prosperity.

www.ingramcontent.com/pod-product-compliance
Lightning Source LLC
LaVergne TN
LVHW051849080426
835512LV00018B/3147